A Heart for Children

D1325751

A Heart for Children

Inspirations for parents and their children

Margaret Fishback Powers

Marshall Pickering
An Imprint of HarperCollins*Publishers*

Marshall Pickering is an Imprint of
HarperCollins*Religious*
Part of HarperCollins*Publishers*
77–85 Fulham Palace Road, London W6 8JB

First published in North America in 1995 by HarperCollins*Publishers* Ltd, Canada
First published in Great Britain
in 1996 by Marshall Pickering

1 3 5 7 9 10 8 6 4 2

The author gratefully acknowledges permission to reprint poems by
Paul L. Powers, Paula Margaret Powers, L. Robbins and Edgar A. Guest.

A catalogue record for this book is
available from the British Library

0 551 030348

Printed and bound in Great Britain by
Woolnough Bookbinding Limited, Irthlingborough, Northamptonshire

Dedicated to my Mom and Dad,
who instilled in me a deep love for literature,
art, music, drama and poetry.

Also to my teachers, Lillian and Ken White,
who carefully taught me the skill of capturing
and making these gifts a natural part of my daily life.

CONTENTS

FOR PARENTS AS TEACHERS

MOTHER LOVE AND FATHER LOVE

THE FAMILY

INTRODUCTION

The subject matter of this collection has taken me on a journey from my childhood through youth, a teaching career, marriage, parenthood and the valleys and glens of life in between. With this book I have tried to share the thoughts of my faith, our Heavenly Father and my dearest Friend, our Lord and Savior Jesus Christ.

As I reflect on some of these poems, the memories almost overwhelm me. With others, I have forgotten just what feeling came over me to put in writing that particular thought, or shadow of a thought. The best that anyone can expect to do is to recombine the experience of the past and compile such impressions as have chimed in with one's own testimony.

Often a few lines have dispelled gloom for me, or soothed troubles. Nothing is so splendid amid serious surroundings as the electric relief of a hearty laugh.

Being a mother was to me a wonder of life. To watch the delicate creations I was allowed to nurture, grow and form personalities, express ideas, communicate with others and, in turn, for them to gradually attempt to share through poetry their inner feelings has been deeply rewarding.

My marriage has always been "a labor of love," as I'm sure my husband of thirty years would agree. If anything, these poems have allowed me to express the joy, fun, frustration and tenderness of our intimacy in faith and hope. Home is where the heart is. My heart has always been with my husband, my family and my faith.

The poems in this volume are filled with the zeal of doing and the joy of living out faith. If it is true that "a friend doubles our joys and halves our sorrows," then it is my prayer that this book should become a friend. I hope its faith and cheer will become a living part of the reader, and the world will be a better place — our friends happier, our homes brighter, and that we become stronger because of our belief that what should be done can be done. One word, one smile, one laugh, one step in faith for tomorrow.

Brighten the corner where you are . . .

Margaret Fishback Powers

FOOTPRINTS

One night I dreamed a dream.
I was walking along the beach with my Lord.
Across the dark sky flashed scenes from my life.
For each scene, I noticed two sets
of footprints in the sand,
one belonging to me
and one to my Lord.
When the last scene of my life shot before me
I looked back at the footprints in the sand.
There was only one set of footprints.
I realized that this was at the lowest
and saddest times of my life.
This always bothered me
and I questioned the Lord
about my dilemma.

"Lord, You told me when I decided to follow You,
You would walk and talk with me all the way.
But I'm aware that during the most troublesome
time of my life there is only one set of footprints.
I just don't understand why, when I needed
        You most,
You leave me."
He whispered, "My precious child,
I love you and will never leave you
never, ever, during your trials and testings.
When you saw only one set of footprints
it was then that I carried you."

◆　　◆　　◆

FOR
PARENTS

———◦(◦)◦———

A HEART FOR CHILDREN

One hundred years from now
It will not matter
What kind of car I drove,
What kind of house I lived in,
How much I had in my bank
Nor what my clothes looked like.

One hundred years from now
It will not matter
What kind of school I attended,
What kind of typewriter I used,
How large or small my church,
But the world may be
. . . a little better because . . .
I was important
in the life
of a child.

TOLERANCE

Could we only see the goodness
Of the ones we meet each day,
We would overlook their failures,
As we greet them on Life's way.

Help me be patient with others' faults;
I know they are patient with me.

❖   ❖   ❖

BABY FEET FOLLOW ME

I cannot name myself as one
Who never goes astray,
Who never stumbles on the road,
Or leaves the hallowed way.
But when I know that baby feet
Will follow where I've trod,
I walk with care that they too may walk
That road that leads to God.

Now as I see my babies bloom
Into young maidens fair
I'll teach and live each day
God's Truth that they can share.

What Goes on Inside

It does not matter too much
What the outside of a boy or girl
looks like, any more than
It matters what the outside
of a house looks like.
It's what goes on inside that counts.

The grandest mansion
In the country
Can be a very unhappy home,
While the simplest cottage
Can be the happiest place
In the world.

♦　　♦　　♦

To Gordon

WHY GOD MADE LITTLE BOYS

God made a world out of His dreams
of majestic mountains, oceans, whispering streams,
golden prairies, rolling plains, and woodland.
Then He paused and thought . . .
I need someone to stand
atop the mountains, to conquer the seas,
explore the plains and climb the trees.
Someone to start out small and grow
sturdy and strong, like a tree, and so . . .
He created boys with adventurous spirit and fun,
to explore and conquer, to romp and run
With dirty faces and banged up chins.
So He did, He completed the task He had begun,
He then stood back and wisely said,
"That's a job well done!"

◆　　◆　　◆

To Christopher Paul

PLUG IN THE BATTERIES

Children are like batteries.
They need a positive
and negative character.
If they are too perfect
they grow up imbalanced;
if they are too acid
society rejects them.
Children need
a Power Source
to show them
how to flow with positive
influences
and to acknowledge
the negative
influences.

Children have abundant
energy, spunk,
spark!
We can channel that energy
to allow them to be used
by the Power Source.

◆　　　◆　　　◆

— Paula Margaret Powers

A NEW BABY GIRL

This is the day
We have been praying for
When God would bless
And open the door
For a new wee soul
To continue
To pour forth love
Overflowing — Sharing needs
for Caring — Crying — Cuddling
Cooing and doing all things
Girls create
In couples.
God bless you and may He enrich your lives.

◆   ◆   ◆

God bless you.

CAN YOU MEASURE A CHILD'S FUTURE?

The line of dots that run up our wall
Tell us our child is growing quite tall;
Shoes that were large now squeeze her toes,
My, how quickly a little child grows.

We are so eager to keep track of her height,
In her physical growth we take such delight;
But spiritual growth, which to God is a treasure,
We might forget, and fail to measure.

More important than inches, or dots on the wall,
Is increasing in wisdom, as Jesus grew tall;
He grew in favor with God and with man,
Will your child do this? With your help, she can!

♦   ♦   ♦

To Christina Michelle

WHEN CHILDREN'S EYES ARE SMILING

When children's eyes are smiling
'Tis God's love that's shining through
With glints of joy and laughter
What good medicine for you!

When children's eyes are smiling
Sure it's Jesus shining through.
Let's all stand up together
And praise His name anew!

When children's eyes are smiling,
When they know the Bible too,
It's a glimpse of His great glory
Heart medicine just for you!

THROUGH THE EYES OF CHILDREN

Through the eyes of children
The world seems bright and gay
The inconsistencies of society
Just seem to drift away.

Through a child's eyes we're not judged
By the color of our skin
But the way one acts . . . conducts oneself
Makes us feel akin.

A child sees the simple things
That we pass by each day,
And views them with a special awe
In very precious ways.

If only we could see our world
The way our children view
We could reach and touch all souls
The way our children do.

◆　　◆　　◆

DISCIPLINE IN LOVE

"Let Johnny do what he wants!
He might get frustrated!" HOGWASH!
On every hand we see the results of "Johnnies"
who are indulged and given their way,
Who have certainly gone astray.
They still want their say
and they are living like bums,
taking no responsibility
for their livelihood or daily funds.
They expect everyone to bow to their wishes
        and commands.
Then they demand obedience with a sneer!
They sometimes burn buildings
and shoot the "pigs" that stop their mayhem,
then, in desperation, find need for them.

The Bible teaches that children
should OBEY their parents.
As the twig is bent so grows the tree
and as children become responsible,
they grow up freely.
Well-mannered and sensitive to others' feelings,
we teach "little people" to show tender dealings.
Children are pliable and teachable,
open and responsive to adults.

"Train up a child in the way he should go;
and when he is old, the narrow way he'll know." *Prov. 22:6*

Obedience is in response to parents
who love and are concerned for their children's
well-being and the end result of consistent
training. (Sometimes, for parents, it's draining!)

Be firm, do not hold back from proper training,
You'll deliver his soul from prison and caning.
Parents, do not provoke your children to wrath
through unfairness or hostility or lack of tact.
Otherwise children become discouraged and resentful —
that's that!
Do not correct your child in anger,
or demand obedience for self-centered reasons . . .
He must continually consider:
"What will make Johnny grow up to be a happy,
well-adjusted Christian man with unblemished page?"
Gently direct him from an early age!
How do you have a HAPPY home?
God loves you and has a wonderful plan
so study God's Word, your true Helping Hand!

◆　　　◆　　　◆

BROKEN DREAMS

As children bring their broken toys
With tears for us to mend,
I brought my broken dreams to God
Because He was my friend.

But then instead of leaving Him
In peace to work alone,
I hung around and tried to help
With ways that were my own.

At last I snatched them back and cried,
"How can You be so slow?"
"My child," He said, "What could I do?
You never did let go."

◆　　　◆　　　◆

THE HEART OF A CHILD

Conscience is never keener
Than it is in childhood.
The history of growth and development
Is one of a gradual hardening of the heart.
Conscience, unless quickened by Christ,
Becomes callused by degrees,
Until in unbelieving old age
There is seldom any distress of heart or mind.
As years pass, people become insensitive to the sin disease.
In childhood a heart is open.

Children are troubled with questions,
And understand deep moral lessons.
They know a sense of guilt from sin,
And are happy to let their Savior come in.
Through forgiveness, God deals with the sin roots
And we can inspect the fruits.
God forgives and forgets, and gives
Blessings eternal and peace of heart.
The tender heart of a child responds
To the sufferings of Christ for sin,
When it is carefully presented to him.
This new child-plant is equally sensitive to love
And learns to give forth love in return.

◆   ◆   ◆

Why God Made Little Girls

God made the world
With its towering trees,
Majestic mountains
And restless seas,
Then paused and said,
"It needs one more thing —
Someone to laugh,
And dance, and sing,
To walk in the woods,
And gather flowers,
To commune with nature
In quiet hours."

So God made little girls
With laughing eyes
And bouncing curls,
With joyful hearts
And infectious smiles,
Enchanting ways
And feminine wiles,
And when He completed
The task He'd begun,
He was pleased and proud
Of the job He'd done.
For the world when seen
Through a little girl's eyes
Greatly resembles Paradise.

◆　　◆　　◆

TAKE TIME

Take time to work,
it is the price of success
Take time to think,
it is the source of power
Take time to play,
it is the secret of youth
Take time to read,
it is the foundation of knowledge
Take time to worship,
it is the highway to reverence
Take time to enjoy friends,
it is the source of happiness
Take time to live,
it is the one sacrament of life
Take time to dream,
it hitches the soul to the stars
Take time to laugh,
it is the support to lift life's load
Take time to pray,
it brings Christ close to you,
And washes life's dirt from your eyes.

◆　◆　◆

Press On

Give me a child whose heart
Is filled with ambition's fire;
Who sets his mark in the start
And keeps moving it higher and higher.
Yes, better to climb and fall
Or sow, though the yield be small,
Than to throw goals away day after day
And never to strive at all.

◆　　◆　　◆

THE SOUL OF A CHILD

The soul of a child is the loveliest flower
That grows in the Garden of God.
Its climb is from weakness to knowledge and power,
To the sky from the clay and the clod.
To beauty and sweetness it grows under care,
neglected, 'tis ragged and wild.
'Tis a plant that is tender, but wondrously rare,
The sweet wistful soul of a child.

Be tender, O Gardener, and give it its share
Of moisture, of warmth, and of light,
And let it not lack for the painstaking care
To protect it from frost and from blight.
A glad day will come when its bloom shall unfold,
It will seem that an angel has smiled,
Reflecting a beauty and sweetness untold
In the sensitive soul of a child.

◆   ◆   ◆

My little cousin had just died. I really tried hard to console the family and ultimately found the words and wisdom while writing this poem.

FOR
CHILDREN

CHILDREN'S PRAYER

Father, we thank You for the night
And for the cheerful morning light,
For rest and food and loving care
And all that makes each day so fair.

Father, we thank You
For Jesus Your Son,
Our best Friend who loves us
Like no other One.

He knows how we're feeling,
Because He was young too,
So we'll trust and obey Him,
The way He did You.

Father, forgive us when we don't do
The things we know You want us to;
Help us forgive others the way You would,
To shine for You, to be strong and good.

In all we do and all we say,
At home and school, at work or play,
Teach us to love, and live by Your way,
To grow more like Jesus each passing day.

❧　　❧　　❧

A Child's Ten Commandments

Thou no gods should have but ME
Before no idol bow the knee
Use not the name of God in vain
Dare not the Sabbath to profane
Give both thy parents honor due
Take heed that thou no murder do
Keep pure and never speak untruth
Steal not, though thou be poor, uncouth
Make not a willful lie nor love it
What is thy neighbor's, do not covet.

◆　　◆　　◆

I Can

Did is a word
of achievement,
Won't is a word
of retreat.
Might is a word
of bereavement,
Can't is a word
of defeat.
Ought is a word
of duty,
Try is a word
for each hour.
Will is a word
of beauty,
Can is a word
of power.
I think I can
I know I can —
The little engine
that tried
then could
and did!

FOR GOD SO LOVED

For God, the Lord of Earth and Heaven,
So Loved, and longed to see forgiven
The World, in sin and pleasure-mad,
That He Gave the greatest gift He had;
His Only Begotten Son, to take our place
That Whosoever, oh, what grace!
Believeth, placing simple trust
In Him, the Righteous and the Just,
Should Not Perish — lost in sin,
But Have Everlasting Life, with Him.

◆　　◆　　◆

WHAT IS CHARITY?

Charity is giving someone a portion of your heart
Charity is longing for them when you're close or far apart . . .

Charity is caring when they're glad and hurting for them
when they are blue
Charity is sharing the good and bad, as though their feelings
were part of you

Charity is memories of happiness in just a touch . . . or flick'ring
smile . . .
Charity is everything that counts; it's what makes life
worthwhile!

◆　　　◆　　　◆

PARENTS

Parents are very special people to each other
and to their children.
Through the years you have shown this to me
By giving me love — by always being there
Whether it be to comfort me in times of need
or to share with me your happiness.
It is such a special feeling
to know that I do have parents as wonderful as you
Whom I love and respect so very much.

And yet —
because feelings are so hard to put into words
I don't tell you often enough how very much I do love you.

◆   ◆   ◆

A WELCOME

The greatest word is God
The deepest word is Soul
The longest word is Eternity
The swiftest word is Time
The nearest word is Now
The darkest word is Sin
The meanest word is Hypocrisy
The broadest word is Truth
The strongest word is Right
The tenderest word is Love
The sweetest word is Home
The dearest word is Friend
The purest word is Savior
The most comforting word is Forgiven
The warmest word is Welcome

◆ ◆ ◆

— Paul L. Powers

He Is the Power

He is the potter
I am the clay
I'm molded from wrong
I'm on the right way.

He is the shepherd
I am the sheep
I'm heeding His voice
To find peace and sweet sleep.

GOD ONLY IS THE MAKER

God alone is the maker
Of all things near and far.
He plants the wayside flower;
He lights the evening star.
The winds and waves obey Him,
By Him the birds are fed,
Much more to us His children
He gives than daily bread.

◆   ◆   ◆

WHO SHOWS THEM

Who shows the little ant the way
Her narrow hole to bore,
And how to spend a summer day
Laying up her winter store?

The sparrow builds her clever nest
Of wool and hay and moss,
Who tells her how to weave it best,
To lay the twigs across?

Who helps the busy bee to fly
Among the sweetest flowers,
And lay her feast of honey by,
To eat in winter hours?

'Tis God who shows them all the way,
And gives them all their skill,
He helps His children as they pray,
To do His holy will.

TOUCH THE CHILD

Touch the child!
Hug away
The hurt.
Wipe away
That tear.
Let the child
Always know
That you
Are there
To care.

◆　　◆　　◆

— Paula Margaret Powers

CAN A LITTLE CHILD LIKE ME

Can a little child like me
Be ready for eternity?
Yes, oh yes, God's Word is true
To tell me what I ought to do:
Obeying God, with all my heart
Accepting His Son, this is the start.

Jesus, we need You
Jesus we love You
Jesus we'll follow Your Word
each day.

Have no other gods but Thee
Nor even make an imagery.
Do not bow to idols — false,
Or serve someone in deceiving cults.
Do not use God's name in vain
To swear, blaspheme or else profane.

❖   ❖   ❖

DEAR TEENS

Can you exist on Earth,
as if there were no Heaven . . .

Can you gain the world,
and in the process, sell your soul . . .

Can you build a future on sand,
when God has given a Solid Rock . . .

Can you live in ease,
while the hungry beg for bread . . .

Can you hoard and store,
when Christ has said share and give . . .

Can you continue to please people,
when it is the Heavenly Father we are to please . . .

Can you stay home in a comfort zone,
when the Savior bids us go . . . ?

When will we give our all,
in order to hear Jesus say . . .

"Well done, thou good and
faithful servant"?

◆   ◆   ◆

— Paul L. Powers

HOW OLD OUGHT I TO BE?

"Dear Mother," said a little maid,
"Please whisper it to me.
Before I am a Christian,
How old ought I to be?"

"How old ought you to be, dear child,
Before you can love me?"
"I've always loved you, Mother, mine,
Since I was a tiny wee.

"I love you now and always will,"
The little daughter said,
And on her mother's shoulder laid
Her golden, curly head.

"How old, my girlie, must you be,
Before you trust my care?"
"Oh, Mother dear, I do, I do —
I trust you everywhere."

"How old ought you to be, my child,
To do the things I say?"
The little girl looked up and said,
"I can do that today."

"Then be a Christian, too.
Don't wait till you are grown.
Tell Jesus now you come to Him
To be His very own."

Then, as the little maid knelt down
And said, "Lord, if I may,
I'd like to be a Christian now,"
He answered, "Yes, today."

◆　　◆　　◆

THANKSGIVING

Be Thankful
for
Jesus
Bibles
Parents
Bread
Night and day
Flowers and trees
Insects and bees
Sunshine and rain
A good heart and brain

◆　　◆　　◆

COMPELLED BY LOVE

To Light my world
to show my love for God
to respect His authority
to live a life of obedience
to be holy as He is holy
to be accountable
to Him.

◆   ◆   ◆

FOR
PARENTS
AS
PARTNERS

MAN AND WOMAN

Woman was made from man's rib
God definitely understood what He did.
She was not created from man's head
To top him, not from his feet
To be stepped upon. Instead —
Woman was made from man's side
To be equal and to always abide
Under his arm, as a bride, protected
from harm —
By him,
For him,
to be a cherished part
forever near to his beating heart.

◆　　◆　　◆

WHAT IS LOVE?

Love is giving someone
A portion of your heart,
Love is thinking of them
When you're close or far apart . . .

Love is caring when they're glad
And caring when they're blue,
Love is sharing good and bad
As though it's part of you . . .

Love is finding happiness
In just a touch or smile,
Love is everything that counts
It's what makes life worthwhile!

◆　　◆　　◆

THE WALL

They say a wife and husband, bit by bit,
Can raise between their lives a mighty wall
So thick they cannot talk with ease
Nor can they see over, for it's so tall!
Its nearness frightens them, but each alone
Is powerless to tear its bulk away
And each one wishes they had known
To such a wall, some magic thing to say!

So let us build with careful art
A bridge of faith between your life and mine,
A bridge of tenderness, and very near
A bridge of understanding strong and fine,
Till we have formed many lovely arcs
And there's no room for walls to rise.

◆　　◆　　◆

APPRECIATION TO MY HUSBAND

I love you because . . .
You're sweet and thoughtful and you are mine;
God gave you to me and I am thine;
Your love is far deeper than surface or time:
God is molding us together with His Love sublime;
Rough edges to share, together God put us in His Wisdom
    Divine;
He destined together we'd work as one and with your name
    I'd sign!

◆　　◆　　◆

Forgiveness (If We Only Knew)

If we only knew that the smiles we see
Often hide tears that fain would be free,
Would we not more tender and loving be,
If only we knew?
If only we knew that the words we say
Oft drive the peace from some heart away,
Would we speak those words in the selfsame way,
If only we knew?
If we only knew that some weary heart
Has been burdened more by our thoughtless art,
Would we cause tears from those eyes to start,
If only we knew?
If we only knew, as we onward go,
Many things that here we can never know,
For more patient love we would often show,
If only we knew.

JOINED TOGETHER

Joined together
Forever on Earth,
Forever in eternity.
Not by the gold ring,
Or the white gown,
The rented tux,
Or flowers.
Not by the groomsmen,
Or bridesmaids,
The pastor's words,
Or candles.

But by the vow of God
Of faithfulness,
Loyalty, and Love —
Through God,
In God,
Married by God,
Forever, for God
To bless.

◆　　◆　　◆

— Paula Margaret Powers

FOR
PARENTS
AS
TEACHERS

CONSEQUENCES

Always watch the words you speak,
Keep them few and sweet;
There may be some bitter words,
You will have to eat.
Don't be too harsh with the child who sins,
To punish unfairly or moan,
Unless you are sure, so
doubly sure,
You have no sins of your own.

◆　　◆　　◆

In appreciation — to a teacher who took time to seek
forgiveness and restoration with a student.

NEVER TOO YOUNG

Too young to know what Christ did
When He hung on Calvary
For parents and children
He cried, "Suffer the 'little people' to come to Me,"
And placed His Hands upon their heads for all to see.
Now children knowing when they're rude and bad
Make Mother and Dad feel angry or sad.
They know when they ought to invite the Savior in
To forgive them for disobedience and their other sins.
It's up to us to show the Way in all that we do and say;
To tell the story of Calvary's Tree so even the youngest one
can see
That Jesus is the Light, the Way.

◆   ◆   ◆

A Teacher's Prayer

God give me wisdom, let me understand,
That I may teach the needful thing;
Help me to see the hidden, struggling child
That I life's rightful messages bring.

God give me patience, for the unending task,
The daily repetitions, the slow years
Of molding, line by line, the human mind
Until at length 'tis free from oppressing fears.

God let me care for those whom I must teach.
Like the Great Teacher, let me love
With tender brooding, and understanding heart,
Eyes wise, far seeing, as the stars above.

God give me faith to see beyond today,
To sow the seed, cultivate the soil;
Then wait serenely, trusting in Thy power
To bless and multiply my humble toil.

◆　　◆　　◆

WITNESSES

Speak the truth to these,
Your precious ones,
Of Christ; tell your daughters
and your sons
Of One who loves them
even more than you;
He will be their Guide
this lifetime through.

◆　　◆　　◆

GENTLE TEACHER

Teach a child
compassion and grace
To judge others
by kindness and honest face
To show by
positive life how to be
To watch him
grow up and then set him free

◆　　◆　　◆

LET ME STAND

I haven't forgotten
What you taught me
In my youth.
I remember
The living lessons
Of daily life —
Of hard times
And close ties.
I know you love me,
And want to protect me —
Forever your little girl.
I know you don't want to lose me —
It is hard to let your child grow up.

But that is the problem
I am no longer a child.

I am still yours,
But a woman now,
With all the longings
And passions
And responses
Of a woman.
I have been trained
In the way I should go
And I won't wander away.
Today I am old enough
And mature enough
And responsible enough
To walk that path
Alone . . .

Or with someone
Of my choice.

Thank you for your help,
Your love and encouragement.
You have worked
All these years
For me
To stand
On my own.

Now,
Let me stand.

◆   ◆   ◆

— Paula Margaret Powers

Burden Bearer

If any little help may ease
The burden of another,
God give me love and care and strength
To help along a brother.

Help me to build people up
Not tear them down.

◆　　◆　　◆

LIFE, WHAT IS IT TO YOU?

To the preacher life's a sermon . . .
to the joker it's a jest;
To the miser life is money . . .
to the loafer life is rest.
To the lawyer life's a trial . . .
to the poet life's a song;
To the doctor life's a patient
who needs treatment right along.

To the soldier life's a battle . . .
to the teacher life's a school;
Life's a "good thing" to the grafter . . .
It's a failure to the fool.
To the man upon the engine
Life's a long and weary grade;
It's chancy to the gambler . . .
to the merchant life's a trade.

Life's a picture to the artist . . .
to the rascal life's a fraud;
Life may be perhaps a burden
to a man beneath the hod;
Life is lovely to the lover . . .
to the player life's a play;
Life may be a load of trouble
to the man upon the dray.

Life's but a long vacation
to the man who loves his work;
Life's an everlasting effort
to the dodger or the shirk;
To the heaven-blest romancer
life's a story, ever new;
Life is what we try to make it . . .
Now, WHAT IS LIFE TO YOU?

◆　　◆　　◆

I WONDER

Year after year they come to me
These children with questioning looks.
Year after year they leave me
As they leave their outgrown books;
And I wonder sometimes if I've taught them
Just some of the worthwhile things,
Just some of the things they'll need in life,
Be they peasants or poets or kings.

Have I taught them the joy of clean living?
That honor is better than fame?
That good friends are the greatest of treasures?
Wealth less than an untarnished name?
Have I taught them respect for the aged?
Protection for those who are weak?
That silence always is golden
When gossip bids them to speak?

Have I taught them that fear is a coward
Who is vanquished on hearing, "I Can"?
That courtesy ranks beside courage
In the heart of a real gentleman?

◆　　◆　　◆

To my teacher, Lillian . . . stirring imagination into the fire
that lights up the dreams of youth, planting the seeds of
character that bloom in great service to mankind.
Telling me, I had great stick-to-it-ive-ness!

MOTHER
LOVE
AND
FATHER
LOVE

MOTHER'S PRAYER

Dear Lord,
May my children grow to be confident,
may they be healthy,
independent adults
caring for themselves
and reaching out to others.
May they have long, successful lives
that grow from failures and errors
I have allowed them to make.
May they have godly, helpful
mates and satisfying careers.
Give me peace and contentment
and when time marches on
help me let them go.

◆   ◆   ◆

Mother's Day

MY MOTHER'S NAME

My husband calls me Mother,
our children as well are proud;
but it reminds me of another
who is soft, sweet and seldom loud.
I love the name of Mother
she's all the world to me.
In all the land there's no other
who's half as sweet as she.
Mother's always loving and kind
and you can be sure I never mind
to sing her praises loud and clear
to shout out, "I love you, Mother, dear."
Her true love no change does know,
Her sensitive side will always show.
She's ready to laugh when you're happy,
Ready to cheer when you're blue.
No matter how far I have to roam

There is certainly no place like home.
I know my Mother's arms yearn
for the time I will again return.
Her voice in memory calls my name,
And Mother-love comfort remains the same.

Something of God is in my Mother's love,
Something of His tenderness and care;
I never see my Mother bent above
An ailing child, but I can see God there.

◆　　◆　　◆

LIFE

God gave me a life in this
body of mine
To have and to hold for
a certain length of time;
So careful I'm being
of this gift, as you see,
My life does not really
belong to me!

◆　　◆　　◆

A Mother's Prayer for Her Unborn

O God, I am looking down to find a soul,
a miracle that shall be mine forevermore,
like no other thing in the world has been mine.
Keep me for my child's life. Bring me through my hour
strong and well for my baby.

Prepare me for motherhood. Shelter my mind
from doubts, worries and misgivings,
that I may not stain my thoughts with cowardice,
for my baby's sake.
Erase all impurities and anger,
low and unworthy feelings from me,
that the little one that is forming may become
a strong, brave body for this world.

As my child looks into my eyes,
may this little one find reverence in me, no fear,
truth and no shame, love strong as life and death,
and no hates or grudges.
Heavenly Father, please make my baby love me. Help me to
    be worthy

to be called to the place of motherhood.
Grant that my child may have a sound mind and a special
      love
for music, art and poetry so that life might be joyful,
relaxing and easy to share with both mother and father.

Abba Father, I will look for my little one's graces and gifts,
and nurture and implant them, so they will grow and develop,
so that this bundle of joy will look up to You in life.
I will try to study and understand my child
throughout life. I promise you, with all my heart,
that the child will find in me faith, fear and reverence
for You, My Heavenly Father.

Please make my baby normal!

◆   ◆   ◆

Rubella scare during pregnancy . . .
A nervous mother-to-be

A TRIBUTE TO MOTHER

For every living sacrifice
you made when I was small,
For all the thoughtful things you did
which no one knew at all,

For all your care and counsel,
for your never-failing cheer,
For all of these I'd like to pay
a fitting tribute here.

But, Mother, any words that I might use
would never, ever do
To tell you half the special thoughts
deep in my heart for you.

And so today, my tribute is
Devotion just the same
and surely too forevermore
the same unchanging love!

◆　　◆　　◆

— L. Robbins

This was written by my late grandmother

FAITH IN LITTLE CHILDREN

Way down deep within your hearts
You're lonesome;
Far within your secret parts
You're lonesome.
Makes no difference how you smile
Where you live or what your style;
You're lonesome.

Tho' your gift of friendship's small
You're lonesome;
Your Mom is looking for your card or call
She's lonesome.
Have faith and love with might and main
Hold out your hands and join the chain;
Your gift will be your crowning joy
When you and Mom are lonesome.

Little ones we love you both
we're lonesome;
You are gems that brightly shine
When we're lonesome.
Some things we just don't understand
But know our Maker's in command;
We're jewels He holds within His hand
When we all are lonesome.

◆　　◆　　◆

May sorrow pass and happiness last.
Dedicated to Margaret and Heather.

A Children's Prayer

For mother-love and father-care,
For brothers strong and sisters fair,
For love at home and here each day,
For guidance lest we go astray,
Father in Heaven, we thank thee.

For the new morning with its light,
For rest and shelter of the night,
For health and food, for love and friends,
For everything His goodness sends,
Father in Heaven, we thank thee.

For flowers that bloom about our feet,
For tender grass, so fresh and sweet,
For all things fair we hear or see,
Father in Heaven, we thank thee.

For blue of stream and blue of sky,
For pleasant shade of branches high,
For fragrant air and cooling breeze,
For beauty of the blooming trees,
Father in Heaven, we thank thee.

◆　　◆　　◆

Thanksgiving for safe arrival
of Christina Michelle

KISSES

It's marvelous what a kiss can do,
A kiss can cheer her when she's blue.
A kiss can say "I love you so"
or "Gee! I hate to see you go."
A kiss is, "Welcome back again"
and "Great to see you" or "Where've you been?"
A kiss can smoothe our small child's pain
And bring a rainbow after rain.
The kiss! There's just no doubt about it,
She scarcely can survive without it.
A kiss delights and warms and charms,
It must be why God gave us arms.
Kisses are great for fathers and mothers,
Sweet for sisters and swell for brothers,
and chances are some favorite aunts
love them more than potted plants.

A kiss can break the language barrier.
No need to fret if mobbed by terrier.
The more you give, the more you get.
So stretch those arms without delay
and give your little girl a kiss today.

◆   ◆   ◆

I penned this message to my husband, Paul.
He felt that perhaps affection would spoil a baby.
He had not been exposed to kisses as a child.

THE GOLDEN BOX

Once upon a Christmastime
Just thirteen years ago
Our little daughter taught Dad
Something he didn't know.
It happened when she got into
Some costly seasonal wrapper;
Its golden glow had caught her eye —
All heaven could not stop her,
From covering her precious gift
With such a special find,
But when he saw what she had done
He nearly lost his mind.

He yelled at her and something more
Of which he was ashamed,
He spanked and yanked that little girl,
Yet he was the one to blame,
For getting mad and making things
More precious than they seem.
For what's more special than a child
More fragile than her dream?
Christmas Day dawned crisp and clear
And gifts were all displayed,
With gleeful joy the golden gift
Into his hands was laid.

As he opened up the box
He could not help but stare.
In disbelief he snapped aloud,
"Why look, there's nothing there!"
Our little girl burst into tears
Saying, "Daddy, that's not true!
You see, I filled it to the top
With kisses just for you!"
Now it was his turn to cry
As he hugged his little sunbeam,
And he learned to trust the ones he loved
'Cause things aren't always what they seem.

Now when he has a trying day
And he's feeling kind of weak
He grabs a kiss out of her box
And plants it on his cheek.
You see, a little girl loved her dad
And taught him something he didn't know
Once upon a Christmastime
Just thirteen years ago.

❖　　❖　　❖

TREASURES

Their bedrooms still hold the sound of whispers and laughter
Yet the kids have long since moved out.
Remembrances of peek-a-boo and pillow-fights;
It brings a tear and a chuckle to me again.
Oh, Lord, our children are truly a Treasure.

I remember trying to sing at their cradle,
Kneeling and listening to prayers before bed.
Mom taught them "Jesus loves me,"
And today, it's still my favorite hymn.
Lord, our children are truly a Treasure.

Their watchful and trusting eyes
Seemed to see in Him a love that others miss.
Lord, may that seed of faith planted so long ago
Grow and go with them as they, too, grow older.
Father, thank you for these Treasures!

◆　　◆　　◆

Fathers, we need to take time to discover
more of these Treasures and enjoy the discovering.

— Paul L. Powers

CONSOLATION

THROUGH THE VALLEY

I have been through the valley of weeping,
Through the valley of sorrow and pain;
But the God of all comfort was with me,
By His hand to uphold and sustain.

When God leads me through valley of trouble,
The design of His will we may trace;
For the trials and sorrows He sends us
Are a part of His infinite grace.

As the earth needs clouds and the sunshine,
So the soul needs sorrow and joy;
And when God puts His gold in the furnace,
He intends all its dross to destroy.

As we travel through life's shadowed valley,
Fresh springs of God's love ever rise,
And we learn that our sorrow and losses
are blessings He sends in disguise.

So I'll follow wherever God leads me,
In the darkness His Word lights my way;
I have proof that the Lord can give comfort,
And His grace can give strength for each day.

Weary toiler, sad and heavy-laden,
Joyfully your great salvation see;
Close beside you stands the Burden-bearer
Strong to bear thy load and thee.

◆　　◆　　◆

On the death of Roy Fishback.
To Lorraine, Ira, Fern and Marie.

EMPTY ARMS

As children filled my daily life
with laughter, singing and tears,
I held my empty arms to God
Because He knew all my fears.
Oh, how my heart and soul were filled
as I felt the motion of my precious one.
I dreamed those nine months ahead
Of the beautiful work He had begun.
In due time your being was complete
And our hearts gave thanks in prayer,
For at last the exciting day arrived
When your birth was announced with a cheer.
You awed us with blue eyes and angel face
As you cuddled in Grandma's powder-blue lace.
Then I heard my Heavenly Father's voice
gently whisper to your wee baby ear . . .
"Now my little one, now my special one . . .
You have paused one precious moment,
and now I have need of you for Myself."
I felt empty arms again.

ANGELS WATCHING OVER YOU

Little boy, little boy,
I snapped on the light of your room
Not guessing it would be the last;
Spotting toys scattered on the floor
Not realizing how suddenly life would pass,
And dreaming we could play just one day more
As I gently and silently shut the door . . .
That bedtime, I tiptoed away
Feeling we would have another day to pray.

Little boy, little boy,
Life for you has gone
God has taken you home from this land of fear
On onionskin angel wings hov'ring near.
Now I stand stooped in sadness with teary eyes
Sorrowing to feel how time flies . . .
While angels watch over you.

◆　　◆　　◆

HIS LOVE

There's a message of Love
Come down from above,
To invite young children to Heaven.
In God's blessed Book
Lost sinners may look
To know how their sins are forgiven.

There they may read
How Jesus the Savior did bleed
And died for the dear little ones.
How clean He can make them,
From the rough to a gem,
And now they're His daughters and sons.

Till, by and by,
He'll take them on High
To be with Him in Heaven's glory,
So close to His heart
They never would part
Children who've believed the Old Story.

◆　　　◆　　　◆

THE LORD IS MY SHEPHERD

In pastures green He leads me
Beside the waters still
And when He blessed and saved me
Never will I lose the thrill.

He restored my soul and made me,
And will lead me for His name's sake,
I know He will never leave me
As He promised never to forsake.

The Shadow of Death hovered over
Yet no evil did I fear
For His sweet voice of comfort
And protection gently came near.

A table in the presence of my enemies,
And my cup runs over with love
As goodness and mercy follow me
I'm covered with God's blessing above.

COMPELLED BY TRUST

May Christ be more at home
in my heavy heart today
As I completely trust in Him
And He dissolves my fears away.
My roots must go down deep
Into the soil of God's Love.
May I feel and understand
How deep and wide . . . how high and low . . .
His love is . . .
To experience this love, myself,
To understand and know
The magnitude of His love.
My cup overflows
And never sees the end
Of His goodness . . .
And may self
Be totally engulfed
In Him.

◆　　　◆　　　◆

GOODBYE

May God, who has chosen this time
To call your loved one to Himself,
Bring you His comfort;
May you rest in the assurance
That His love is upon you
To direct you in His perfect plan.

Some boys are like fine crystal; too fragile for this world, but just right for His.

◆   ◆   ◆

DOES EVERY PRAYER COUNT FOR TWO?

Does every prayer count for two
If I say that prayer for you?
Will Jesus listen extra close
To grant you special blessings' dose?
If I were God I'd not be fair
Because I'd give you treasures rare —
I'd want for you the best of life
So I'd lift you o'er the strife.
I'd never allow ANY pain —
Always sunshine, never rain!
But strife brings faith, pain brings hope,
And I know God helps you cope.
And so I feel God's ways are best
And in Him, I'll let you rest.
Remember this — I love you true
And don't forget I pray for you.

◆   ◆   ◆

— Paula Margaret Powers

INSPIRATIONS

A Prayer

Lord, let the glow of Your love
Through my whole being shine
Fill me with gladness from above
and hold me by strength Divine
Lord, make Your Light in my Heart
Glow radiant and clear, never to part.

◆　　◆　　◆

TURN TO HIM

Life is filled with troubles
Caused by man's sin,
When we find peace in Jesus
Our troubles seem to dim.

Life is filled with heartaches
To drop at the Savior's feet,
He will give us contentment
And all our problems meet.

Life is filled with laughter
As the sun shines bright,
When we depend on His goodness
He'll keep our ship aright.

Life is filled with pleasures
When we follow in His footsteps,
And he turns the night to day
And keeps us from the depths.

Life is filled with traveling
As o'er the globe we roam,
But with all the seven wonders,
There's still no place like home.

◆　　◆　　◆

OUR CHOICE

Not what we have, but what we use,
Not what we see, but what we choose;
These are the things that mar or bless
The sum of human happiness.

The thing nearby, not that afar,
Not what we seem, but what we are;
These are the things that make or break,
That give the heart its joy or ache.

Not what seems fair, but what is true,
Not what we dream, but good we do;
These are the things that shine like gems,
Like stars in Fortune's diadems.

Not as we take, but as we give,
Not as we pray, but as we live;
These are the things that make for peace,
Both now and after time shall cease.

I F

If you think you are beaten — you are
If you think you dare not — you don't
Success begins with your own will . . .
It's all in your state of mind.
Life's battles are not always won
By those who are stronger or faster;
Sooner or later the person who wins
Is the person who thinks they can.
If they never give up
If they never give in,
If they never quit
If they try
and try
and try again.

DON'T QUIT

When things go wrong, as they sometimes will,
When the road you're trudging seems all uphill,
When the funds are low and the debts are high,
And you want to smile, but you have to sigh,
When care is pressing you down a bit —
Rest if you must, but don't you quit.
Life is queer with its twists and turns
As everyone of us sometimes learns
When they might have won had they stuck it out,
Don't give up though the pace seems slow —
You may succeed with another blow.

Often the struggler has given up
When he might have captured the visitor's cup;
And he learned too late when the night came down
How close he was to the golden crown,
Success is failure turned inside out —
So stick to the fight when you're hardest hit —
It's when things seem worst that
You mustn't quit.

◆   ◆   ◆

— Edgar A. Guest
A gift to Margaret Rose Fishbach

THE LORD BLESS THEE

How shall He bless thee?
With the gladness that knoweth no decay,
With riches that cannot pass away,
With the sunshine that makes an endless day,
Thus may He bless thee!
How shall He keep thee?
In the all-covering shadow of His wings,
With the strong love that guards from evil things,
With the sure power that safe to glory brings,
Thus may He keep thee!
How shall He give thee joy?
With God first in thy life. Love Him,
Trust Him, obey Him, to be assured
of joyful, fruitful living, never lured
away from the Bible promises. The Lord endured
and shall continually guide thee!

POINT OF VIEW

A traveler stopped at a busy hour
By a busy thoroughfare,
To ask of a busy construction crew
What person employed them there.
Said the "first human ant" when
accosted thus,
His helmet awry on his head,
"I work for a pittance, compared with the boss,
I slave for my daily bread."
Said the second, his hat obscuring his view
where ennui and self-pity admixt,
"I put in eight hours each day on the job
just toting my quota of bricks."
But the third man looked up from his
labor at the bench
And said with a light in his eyes,
"With the help of my toil, on this
fortunate sight
A temple of God will arise."

◆　◆　◆

To Dad Fishbach

FREE

Speak to us, Lord, till shamed
by Thy great giving
That our hands unclasp
to set our treasures free;
Our wills, our love, our possessions
All gladly yielded up,
gracious Lord, to Thee.
Not in having or receiving,
But in giving there is bliss;
He who has no other pleasure,
May evermore rejoice in this.

◆　　◆　　◆

Time Management

If your work is at once begun
Never leave it till it's done;
Be the labor great or small
Do it well or not at all.
If over and over God deigns to work
Why should we faint, one duty shirk?
So over and over our tasks we do
Sure of reward if our work be true.
I have a strength to keep me true
And straight in everything I do;
I have a power to keep me strong
When I am tempted to do wrong.

Redeem the time! God only knows
How soon our little life may close,
With all its pleasures and its woes.
Redeem the time! Time management grows.
Live neither in the past nor in the future
But let each day's work absorb all
Your interest, energy and enthusiasm.
The best preparation for tomorrow
is to do today's work superbly well . . .

Did you waste the day or lose it?
Was it well or poorly spent?
Did you leave a trail of kindness
Or a scar of discontent?

◆   ◆   ◆

LISTEN TO THE CHILDREN

"Good Shepherd, we've been caring
For the lambs you send our way,
We pray that at eventide
You'll be pleased to say
'Well done!'

"Good Shepherd, we've been feeding
Little lambs in lands near and far
Both in cities and the outback
Under sun and glittering star,
We hear, 'Well done!'

"Good Shepherd, listen to children
Crying in hunger and pain
Give them strength and healing
To hear Your words of comfort
'I have given My life for you
Rest in Me.'"

◆　　◆　　◆

QUALIFICATIONS

A bigger place than this to fill
For that I do not pray,
But to be big enough to fill
The place I have today.

Don't be disheartened, God is always in the midst of
your trivial and seemingly unsolvable problems.
He is the Answer.

◆   ◆   ◆

TREASURES OF THE HEART

Rich treasures in the goldmine of life
We're called to dig up ourselves,
It seems a miner faces strife
As lethargy each man fells.

Rich nuggets of gold and silver
Now hold no attraction for me,
And diamond, garnet and sapphire
Are not the treasures I see.

Rich treasure in the goldmine of life
Is the gemstone called "a soul,"
Cut by trials as sharp as a knife.
God help me see past the coal.

◆　　◆　　◆

SUNSHINE AND MUSIC

A laughter is just like sunshine,
It freshens all the day,
It tips the peak of life with light,
And drives the clouds away;
The soul grows glad that hears it,
And feels its courage strong;
A laugh is just like sunshine
For cheering folks along.

A laugh is just like music,
It lingers in the heart,
And where its melody is heard
The ills of life depart
And happy thoughts come crowding
Its joyful notes to greet;
A laugh is just like music
For making living sweet.

BURDENS

Burdens of life are many
Some great and some small —
But no matter your problem
He can take care of them all.

Just cast your burdens on Jesus
The answer you can find —
Tho' life might fail you
He's there all the time.

Burdens begin to grow smaller
Tho' the way is rough, and drear,
As we call on Jesus our Savior
He again makes the path so clear.

Never forget the Master
As you travel from day to day —
And no matter how big your problem
His Unseen Presence can ease it away.

◆　　◆　　◆

VICTOR

His be the Victor's name,
Who fought the fight alone!
Triumphant saints no honor claim
His conquest was His own.

Though weakness and defeat
He won Rod, Staff and Crown;
Trod all our foes beneath His feet
By being trodden down.

Bless, bless the Conqueror slain —
Slain in His victory.
He lived; He died; He lives again
For saints, His Church, for thee.

HAVE FAITH

When troubles and trials are near
And death claims someone so dear,
When you are lonely and sad
Or things happen to make you glad;
When finances are low
And your children still grow,
When you're out of food
And the taxes are due,
Or when things are great
And you love your mate,
Have faith,
Ask the Savior to walk by your side
To prepare your path
with Him to abide.

◆　　◆　　◆

THE
FAMILY

———◦◦◉◦◦———

OUR FAMILY

Our family is a blessing
It means so many things
Words could never really tell
the joy our family brings.
Our family is a mutual love
the love of father and mother
Showing children how to love
and care for one another.
Our family is heartfelt pride
the feeling deep and strong
that makes us glad to take a part
and know that we belong.

Our family is always home
no matter how far we roam.
We can share our joys and sorrows
hopes and dreams
for happiness lives there.
Our family is a bond of faith
that even time can't sever.
A gift to last throughout our lives
For the family of God is forever.

❖　　❖　　❖

WE BELIEVE IN CHILDREN

We believe the children to be the future
of our land;
So teach them well and take them gently
by the hand.
Show them all the beauty they possess
inside,
Try to make life easier by giving them
"sense of pride."
Let the Little People's music and laughter
ring out;
By your own life, walk and talk — don't let
them doubt.
We believe the children to be the future
of our land;
We know He won't forget them . . . He has
carved them on the palm of His hand.

❖　　❖　　❖

FAMILY INHERITANCE

He has blessed us abundantly
with love, peace and joy
through His Holy Spirit.
He has blessed us with strength,
upholding us so that we
do not sink or slide.
He is completing in us daily
a good work and helping us
not to hide.
He is calming our storm
and comforting us when we mourn.
He is drying our tears
and relieving our fears.
He will never leave us
nor forsake us.

THE FAMILY'S TREK

They say the majesty of God
Is found on mountaintops,
But we can see the power of Him
In the morning's new dewdrops.
We can see Yahweh's strength
Within the wind-bent reed,
And can feel His unfolding plan
Tucked in the mustard seed.

And if He has such a plan
For the flower and the tree,
How much more has He set
Along life's path for me?
How can we doubt the wisdom
Of such a careful hand,
Who always sets our feet on rock
And not on shifting sand?
God's loving Hand has led us
On up and downhill road —
He provides for all our needs
And carries our life's load.

◆　　◆　　◆

— Paula Margaret Powers

FAMILY COMMUNICATION GUIDELINES

Be a ready listener,
and do not answer until the other person
has finished talking. *Prov. 18:13*

Be slow to speak. Think first,
then use your verse. Don't be hasty in your words,
but speak in such a way that the other person
can understand and accept what you say. *Prov. 15:23*

Speak the truth always,
but do it in love. Do not exaggerate! *Eph. 4:15*

Do not use silence
to frustrate the other person. Explain why
you are hesitant to talk at this time.

Do not become involved in quarrels.
It is possible to disagree without quarrelling. *Prov. 17:14*

Do not respond in anger.
Use a soft and kind response. *Prov. 14:29*

When in the wrong, admit it,
and ask for forgiveness. When someone confesses to you,
tell them you forgive them.
Be sure it is FORGOTTEN and not brought up to the
person. *Prov. 17:9*

Avoid nagging! *Prov. 10:19*

Do not blame or criticize others,
but restore them, encourage them, and edify them.
If someone verbally attacks, or criticizes or blames you,
do not respond in the same manner. *Rom. 12:17*

Try to understand
the other person's opinion.
Make allowances for differences. Be concerned
about their interests. *Phil. 2:1-4*

Remember
When the FAMILY breaks down . . .
The most important Institution of our Nation breaks down!
Let's keep those communication lines OPEN!

◆   ◆   ◆

HOME

Home to laughter, home to rest,
Home to those that we love best,
Home to where there is none to hate,
Where no foes in anguish wait,
Where no jealous envious mind
Seeks with glee a fault to find.
Now the day is done and I
Turn to hear a welcoming cry.
Love is dancing at the door,
I am safe at home once more.

◆　　◆　　◆

THE FAMILY

A Man and a Woman have become one before our Holy God.
Both will need to make many
Adjustments in their lives to live
To achieve harmony in the home.
Together they will instruct in Love
and prepare their youth for Life.
With much prayer and petitions
before the Lord
for their Youth
to bring them up
in the nurture and honor
of God our Father.

◆   ◆   ◆